W9-BUJ-023

Failure is not Final

The Art of Stepping Out in Faith

Roger Hernández

Pacific Press®
Publishing Association

Nampa, Idaho | Oshawa, Ontario, Canada
www.pacificpress.com

Cover design by Steve Lanto
Cover resources from iStockphoto.com
Inside design by Kristin Hansen-Mellish

Copyright © 2013 by Pacific Press® Publishing Association
Printed in the United States of America
All rights reserved

Unless otherwise indicated, all Scripture quotations are taken from the
Holy Bible, New Living Translation, copyright © 1996, 2004, 2007
by Tyndale House Foundation. Used by permission of Tyndale House
Publishers, Inc., Carol Stream, Illinois 60188. All rights reserved.
Scripture quotations marked NIV are taken from the HOLY BIBLE,
NEW INTERNATIONAL VERSION®. Copyright © 1973, 1978,
1984 by International Bible Society. Used by permission of Zondervan
Publishing House.
Scripture quotations marked CEV are from the Contemporary English
Version. Copyright © American Bible Society 1991, 1995 Used by
permission.

The author assumes full responsibility for the accuracy of all facts and
quotations as cited in this book.

Additional copies of this book may be obtained by calling toll-free
1-800-765-6955 or online at http://www.adventistbookcenter.com.

Library of Congress Cataloging-in-Publication Data:
Hernandez, Roger, 1967-
  Failure is not final : the art of stepping out in faith / Roger Hernandez.
     pages cm
  ISBN 13: 978-0-8163-4946-3 (pbk.)
  ISBN 10: 0-8163-4946-0 (pbk.)
1. Failure (Psychology)—Religious aspects—Christianity. I. Title.
  BT730.5.H47 2013
  248.8'6—dc23
                                    2013036650

December 2013

Dedication

To my wife, Kathy: you have been there in my greatest failures and my most pleasing successes.

To my friends Kendall, Walters, and Jose: large distances separate us, but you are never far.

To my Savior and Lord Jesus Christ: You turned it around.

Contents

Understanding the Reasons We Fail

Understanding the Opportunities and Lessons Failure Affords Us

Understanding the Importance of How We React in the Recovery From Failure

Introduction

Everyone loves a winner. We name our daughters Victoria and our sons Victor. I can't recall ever being introduced by a parent to children named Loser Smith and Defeated Martinez. When the team that we like to follow wins, we declare boldly, "We won," even though we had no active part on the field of play. A cursory search of the Web about sports teams shows that many more fans follow the Cowboys, Yankees, and Lakers than the Bucs, Pirates, and the Blazers. Why? The former have a track history of winning. Love them or hate them, winners are more popular.

Although we have this fascination with and desire for success, the reality is that we have failed many more times than we care to admit or even remember.

- Failed marriages and business ventures
- Failed attempts to complete an education
- Poor choices have left you in failing health
- Less than desirable results in your relationship with your children or parents

For some, a career choice is not panning out. Perhaps you're a pastor in a declining church. Maybe a downturn in the economy tanked your investments. An idea that looked great when first conceived has not worked. Whatever field you are in, you will at some time or other experience failure.

The question becomes, what can I do when I experience failure? You probably fall into one of the three groups of people who are reading this book:

- Some are about to enter into a season of failure. They can see it coming. This book may be able to prevent or shorten it.
- Some are smack-dab in the middle of a failure. The principles contained in these pages can shed some light on the situation and teach valuable lessons while showing a way to recover.
- Some are on the other side. Failure is in the rearview mirror, and they are on the road to a better situation.

My desire is that you stay on that road for as long as you can!

This book is divided into three parts: (1) Why? (2) What? (3) How? We will examine *why* we fail. Then we will take a look at *what* lessons we can learn from failure. To conclude, we will study *how* we react to failure. Let's get started.

Part one
Why?

Understanding the Reasons We Fail

Reasons for failure

Chuck Swindoll tells a story about Chippy. Chippy was a happy bird that lived with his owner. He loved to sing from his cage. He was well fed and his owner took good care of him. Life was grand. Then one day, it all went awry. The owner wanted to clean Chippy's cage, so she turned on the vacuum cleaner, and after connecting the extension hose, proceeded to vacuum the bottom of Chippy's cage. At that moment the phone rang. The owner tried to do two things at the same time. With her left hand she continued to vacuum the cage, and with her right hand she answered the phone. She got distracted, and before she knew it she had vacuumed up Chippy. Immediately, she opened the bag and found Chippy, stunned but alive and covered with dust.

Horrified at what she had done, she grabbed Chippy and put him under the shower head, turning on the water full blast. Realizing that the cure was worse than the problem, she grabbed him and put him on the bathroom counter. She turned the hairdryer on high and pointed it at him to dry him off. Chippy survived, barely. Someone asked the owner about Chippy some time later, and the owner said, "Chippy doesn't sing much anymore."

We all fail. We have all had one of those days when nothing goes as planned. Have you ever felt like Chippy? I know I have.

When failure comes, one important question we should ask ourselves is *Why*? Most of the time we can discover the answer to that question. The Bible mentions several reasons *why* people fail. Let's look at three of them.

Reason 1—Disconnecting

"And now, O our God, what can we say after all of this?
For once again we
have abandoned your commands!"
—*Ezra 9:10*

The first reason the Bible gives for failure is disconnecting from God.

Before we continue, however, we must make one thing clear. Our salvation is by grace alone, through faith alone, period. We don't deserve it, can't earn it, and will never be good enough to merit it.

That being said, there are many biblical examples of the connection between obedience and blessing, as well as the connection of willful disobedience and failure. Not every person who disconnects from God will experience failure immediately, but most people who experience constant, sustained failure have disconnected from God at some point in their lives.

Maybe now your life isn't so great. Perhaps, neither Plan A, B, or C has panned out. In fact, you've run out of letters in the alphabet and have started to use numbers. Maybe everything you touch seems to turn into dust, not gold. Crisis is your middle name, and drama, issues, and problems are your constant companions. If you are experiencing failure right now, I invite you to examine your relationship with God *first*. The further away from God that you are, the closer you are to failure.

The Bible mentions several benefits of a strong spiritual connection with God. These benefits contribute to our well-being, and their absence can make our lives less than ideal. Here are three.

1. Guidance. Second Chronicles 26:5 says, "Uzziah sought God during the days of Zechariah, who taught him to fear God. And as long as the king sought guidance from the LORD, God gave him success."

Human beings are often affected by their past and worried about their future, which disturbs their present. God is different. He erases our yesterdays, is in charge of our tomorrows, and brings peace to our todays, because He is guiding us. Having a supernatural GPS is not only important, it is necessary for success.

2. Support. Job 4:4 tells us, "Your words have supported those who were falling; you encouraged those with shaky knees."

Sometimes, things get so rough that you just need someone to say, "Everything will be OK." One of my favorite books in the Bible is the book of Psalms. I can't count the times that I have gone to that section of the

Bible and read a psalm that's had a physically and emotionally positive effect on me. God's Word does, in fact, support, encourage, and sustain us through hard times.

You will encounter three types of people when you are going through tough times:

- Those who can help you but choose not to.
- Those who can't help you but would like to.
- Those who can help you and want to.

Only God fits in the third category every time.

3. Perspective. Job 23:14 says, "He will do to me whatever he has planned. He controls my destiny."

One of the most basic, yet often forgotten, truths of Scripture is that God is God and I am not. As I read the Bible, I am reminded of that fact, and it makes all the difference in the world. Our perspective is often skewed by our sinfulness and our myopic understanding of the grand scheme of things. God continually reminds us that He has a plan, His plan is better than ours, and His plan will succeed at the end. As you go through difficult situations, following God's principles will help you catch a glimpse of the bigger picture. Remember,

- Just because you don't feel Him, doesn't mean He is not real.
- Just because you don't see Him work, doesn't mean He isn't working for you.

Why?

- Just because you don't agree with His plan, doesn't mean it's not the right one.

A couple was driving down a country road on a crisp autumn afternoon. It was during the 1970s, when many cars had wide, unobstructed bench seats. The wife looked at her husband from the passenger side and said to him, "Honey, I feel that we have grown apart. I remember when we were dating, even newlyweds, we used to ride in this same car very close to each other. Now look at us. You're on one side and I'm way on the other. What happened to us?" The husband, without missing a beat, said, "If you feel we have grown apart, ask yourself, Who moved?"

If you feel that the distance between you and God has increased, ask yourself, Who moved?

Reason 2—Shortcuts

Good planning and hard work lead to prosperity,
but hasty shortcuts lead to poverty.
—Proverbs 21:5

The second reason why people fail is that they take shortcuts. Shortcuts are a method people use to try to accomplish more tasks in less time. But there are some things in life that we can't rush. Patience is not like fast food; it is more like Thanksgiving dinner. (If you have fast food for Thanksgiving, skip this section!)

I am an impatient person by nature. Can you relate? I despise waiting in line, I hate the three-day waiting period, and being stuck in traffic elevates my stress levels. The temptation for people like me, and I suppose many others, is to take shortcuts to accomplish our goals. I want things to move faster, people to change more quickly, and problems to be resolved in an instant.

Inventors are coming up constantly with new contraptions to make our lives easier. A while back, I read a study done decades ago, which projected that in the 1980s, people would work fewer hours, have more free time, and have an easier life because of all the coming time-saving inventions. The exact opposite has happened! Even with all our advances, we are still looking for less complicated lives, but find disappointment instead.

There is a direct connection between impatience and taking shortcuts, for taking shortcuts is the external manifestation of an internal reality. A biblical principle that has helped me deal with my impatience is this:

> You can't do much to accelerate God's blessing, but you can do a lot to delay it.

The Bible speaks about "the appointed time" and "a time and a season for everything." Timing is everything as we deal with spiritual issues. One of the clearest examples of this principle is the journey that the people of Israel took from Egypt to the Promised Land. A reading of the last chapters of Genesis as well as the book of Exodus will show the danger of impatience. A journey that should have taken *days* took *decades*. Why? Impatience and a bad attitude. Every time the Israelites said, "We don't like our leaders," God said, "One more time around the desert." Every time they complained about the water, the food, or anything else, God said, "One more time." The truth is that one of the fastest ways to delay your blessing is a bad attitude. It makes us say things such as:

- Why couldn't I have married her/him?
- Why won't God bless me?
- Why don't my kids behave like those children?
- Why is he in that position and I am not?
- Why did she get married and I'm still single? I mean, God, have you *seen* her?

You know how God responds? "One more time . . ." If your life seems to be stuck in the desert, and you are moving but not really going anywhere, one of the first things to check would be your attitude. If your attitude is one of impatience, a correction needs to be made immediately. Don't get me wrong. There are times when we must act decisively, when we must go forward in

Jesus' name. But a lot of damage has been done because

- we moved ahead without godly consensus;
- we left before it was time; and
- we started a project without God's blessing.

Don't confuse activity with progress. We confuse movement with advancement, action with success, and program implementation with personal growth. The question is not whether we have things going on, but whether God is leading.

In my twenty years as a minister, I have seen people fail in three areas because of impatience and shortcuts:

1. Relationships. Loneliness can mess with your mind. I understand it's tough to see all your friends getting married while you are still single. But rushing into a relationship can be devastating. If you feel lonely, get a dog. Don't rush into love.

2. Finances. There is no such thing as a get-rich-quick strategy. In fact, a study of lottery winners demonstrated that many were left without a penny only a short time after winning millions. Trying to invest in pyramid schemes, or lacking research before beginning a financial venture, can leave you penniless and distraught.

3. Moving. Later on I'll go into more detail about the desire that some have to leave a situation every time things get a little rough. For now, let me just say that the temptation to flee is a real one, especially when things aren't going so great. Be careful that you are not running from what seems like an external situation, when, in fact, the problem might be internal. No matter where you run, an internal problem will follow you there.

Only God's power can sustain you for the long haul, so be patient.

Underneath impatience lies a desire for control. The reason we take shortcuts and end up failing is that we think *we* know best. The truth is, we don't. Relinquish everything to God.

In your life there are things that

- you will never change—leave those alone;
- will change slowly—have patience; and
- need changing now—have courage.

The key is to have the divine gift of discernment, to know which is which.

I like to work around the house. I like to repair, rebuild, restore, demolish, rearrange—you know, your weekend-warrior type of remodeling. There's only one problem. I'm not good at it. If I had to earn a living as a handyman, I would die of hunger. That's the reason I invite my brother-in-law to come work with me in my "projects." After all, I introduced him to his wife, so he owes me. He is really good at remodeling. You could say he was born with a hammer in his hand and probably remodeled his own crib. He is very detail oriented (I'm not), likes to take his time (I don't), and doesn't take shortcuts (I do). One of my favorite expressions I say to try to get him to work faster is, "You can't see that detail from a helicopter." He just ignores me and continues to work. When it's all done and I look at the finished product, I'm glad we took our time. A couple of times, however, we've done it my way, and some sections of my house are a constant reminder of the fallacy of shortcuts. In life, as in construction, it's better to measure twice and cut once.

Reason 3—Pride

Pride ends in humiliation, while humility brings honor.
—Proverbs 29:23

The three most dangerous words in the English language are "I already know." I have a teenage son who learned those words early, probably from his mother (or me, but who's keeping track, right?). He loves to tell me how well he can fix, do, complete, and perform any task known to man. I try to be patient with him, because I remember that I was the same way at that age, and because I love him dearly. But to be totally honest, it's hard!

The third reason why people find themselves in the midst of failure is their pride. There is nothing wrong with being a confident person. In fact, a truly confident person will be smart enough to recognize that he doesn't know it all, can't do it all, and needs the help of God and other people to be successful. Being teachable and admitting our mistakes is not a sign of weakness but of true strength. Pride leads to failure in the following ways:

1. Hard to live with. No one likes a know-it-all. I don't think that type of person even likes himself! The greater the pride, the harder it is for others to relate to him. Pride damages relationships with others in these ways:

- It makes you act superior, alienating others.
- It makes you incapable of admitting wrongs, frustrating others.
- It makes you a person who does not listen well, distancing others.

Pride is rooted in a distorted view of self. Some people with a low self-image try to overcompensate by acting in prideful ways. This only serves to distance them from others, especially from loved ones. One of the things I counsel parents to do is admit to their kids when they have made a mistake. Contrary to popular belief, that admission strengthens your bond; it does not make you weaker. The apostle Paul had it right when he wrote in Romans 12:16, "Live in harmony with each other. Don't be too proud to enjoy the company of ordinary people. And don't think you know it all!"

2. Harder to be blessed. One of the fastest ways of

stopping your life's momentum is to believe your own press clippings. The temptation to take some of God's glory for yourself, even if it is disguised in pious statements, will carry grave consequences. God will not share His glory with us. If you sense that momentum has slowed down or stopped in your life, one of the first questions I would ask is the following: Is God getting all the glory? One of the texts that brings out this powerful truth is James 4:6. "He gives us . . . more grace to stand against such evil desires. As the Scriptures say, 'God opposes the proud but favors the humble.' "

Sometimes I have heard people blame the devil for their lack of personal growth and success when, in fact, it could be God who is slowing them down. Maybe it's just me, but with all the opposition we can face these days, do we need to add *God* to that list? I think not.

3. Hardest to follow. You may be a leader. An effective leader admits he does not know everything. Followers want to feel that they are contributing to the overall well-being of the company/organization. A prideful attitude alienates followers and fosters discontent and turnover. Healthy leaders have the ability to recognize that they don't know it all, and they surround themselves with people who can make up for those deficiencies.

Admitting your weakness makes your leadership stronger. "Never let them see you sweat" is a good slogan for a deodorant but not for a leader. A leader once said, "Without wise leadership, a nation falls; there is safety in having many advisers" (Proverbs 11:14).

I'm a sports fanatic. I follow the Cowboys, the Yankees, and any soccer team that is *not* Argentina. One of the key questions professional athletes have to ask themselves is, "When should I retire?" Very seldom do you see a professional athlete realize by him- or herself that the time has come, without the help of being benched or cut from the team. The reason? Pride. It's very hard to admit that you can't do it anymore. There's somebody younger, faster, and better than you. Pride clouds and distorts the true picture of self, which is why it's important to surround ourselves with "no men," not just "yes men."

The Bible is clear when speaking about pride. It precedes nothing that is good, and it is a precursor to failure. Proverbs 16:18 says, "Pride goes before destruction, and haughtiness before a fall."

Today, listen to God speaking to you and telling you that

- you have nothing to prove, love Me instead;
- you cannot impress Me, worship Me instead; and
- you don't know, trust Me instead.

Part two
What?

Understanding the Opportunities and Lessons Failure Affords Us

Opportunities from failure

One of my favorite examples of a person who learned from his failure is Thomas Edison. He's best known for inventing the light bulb, but he did so after many failed attempts. Sometimes the filaments were too thick and the light bulb exploded. Other times it was too thin and it wouldn't light up. After each failed experiment, he learned what not to do, until he finally discovered the perfect combination.

Failure is not final. Failure brings a great opportunity for us to learn and grow. Failure that we learn from is no longer a failure; it is a lessoned learned. The Bible presents three opportunities that are afforded to us through failure.

Opportunity 1—Failure reveals our problems

People who conceal their sins will not prosper,
but if they confess and turn from them, they will
receive mercy.
—Proverbs 28:13

The first opportunity that we have when we fail is to take stock of our lives. Failure is a great teacher, although many times we don't like to take that class. I believe that sometimes we learn more by failure than by success. When we always win, the only thing we learn is to be prideful. Failure is like a bright sticky arrow pasted on a document that says, "Pay attention to this." Even though God is not interested in bringing us unnecessary pain, He can use failure to point out glaring weaknesses and areas of needed growth in our lives.

I regularly meet with people for pastoral counseling and find two types of people. The people in one group fail, learn from the failure, and grow. Those in the other group also fail but learn nothing from it and repeat the failure. Here are some real-life examples:

A woman starts a relationship with a man. He proves to be a controlling, even abusive partner. She finds out that he is running around with other women. Frustrated, she ends the relationship, sometimes not soon enough, and changes her Facebook status to "It's complicated." After a while, loneliness strikes, and after a phone call, the two are back together. The cycle of dysfunction, of breaking up and making up, goes on and on. Sometimes it goes even further: the woman gets into a different relationship with a different man but with the same results. While it is important not to blame the victim here, doesn't it make sense after three failed relationships with the same characteristics to take a good hard look at oneself and ask the difficult questions:

- Why am I so attracted to less-than-ideal men?

What?

- What is it about me that attracts them?
- What changes in my character are necessary to have better relationships?

A man gets a job. It's not his ideal job, but it pays the bills, of which he has many. Since he does not like his job or his boss, he puts very little effort into the work. His lack of teamwork and support is noticed by his superiors. He is given a written notice of a less-than-stellar performance review, which he ignores. Several weeks later, another notice comes, this one with a pink slip attached to it. When asked about his employment status, he tells people close to him that he is "in between jobs" and mumbles something about how bad the economy is and all the good jobs are taken. Before he fills out yet another unemployment application, he should ask himself:

- Why do I keep getting fired?
- What action steps do I need to take so that this doesn't happen in my next job?
- What training can I receive, what materials can I read, what events can I attend that would improve my effectiveness as an employee?

A couple starts attending a new church. They are eager to get involved and immediately get busy. There's just one problem. They are hypersensitive. Any comment that has the slightest hint of criticism or displeasure in it creates an immediate and powerful reaction. After several blowups, they leave the church in a stampede, but not before letting everyone within earshot know about the church's lack of love and support, and they go on to the next church, where the cycle begins all over again. Before they ask the church clerk for their membership transfer, they should ask themselves the following questions:

- How's my spiritual connection with God?
- Am I clear on the reason why I serve?
- Why do I run away from conflict?

A teenager gets his research paper back from the teacher. Not a lot of work and effort went into it, and the grade reflects that fact. Later that day, before the paper is seen by his parents, he gives an explanation—the teacher discriminates and shows favoritism toward other students. The parents listen and agree, reinforcing in the student the unfortunate victim mentality that no matter what happens, it's never your fault. Before the next assignment is due, wouldn't it be smart for the teenager to examine his previous performance and ask:

- Is this discrimination or lack of effort?
- Is it favoritism or shoddy work?

What?

- Did I give it my all or was it a last-minute effort?

These cases might seem stereotypical, but they happen in real life. Whenever we are staring at failure face to face, we need to ask ourselves: Why did I fail? And then we must learn from the failure.

Why is it important to learn from our failures? Here are three reasons.

1. Demonstrates our intelligence. Proverbs 18:15 says, "Intelligent people are always ready to learn. Their ears are open for knowledge."

It may seem strange, but we demonstrate our intelligence by admitting that we are not that smart and don't know it all! Someone has said that the definition of a crazy person is one who repeats the same action time after time, expecting different results. A smart person analyzes his mistakes looking for learning opportunities and, after failing, becomes wiser, having learned from the experience. Nothing exemplifies a smart person better than one who learns the lesson the first time.

2. Impacts our behavior. Psalm 119:7 tells us, "As I learn your righteous regulations, I will thank you by living as I should!"

Failure is a great teacher. One lesson we learn is that deficiencies in our character affect our behavior. Failure is a great way to find out where your growth areas are, and we all have them. For example, behind most failed relationships are bad decisions that were motivated by character flaws and expressed in less-than-ideal actions. When we learn from failure, we grow, and that helps us to think twice before we make the same mistakes.

3. Brings honor to our lives. Finally, Proverbs 1:9 teaches us, "What you learn from them will crown you with grace and be a chain of honor around your neck."

How do you describe an honorable person? According to this particular text, that title belongs to someone who is willing to learn from others, including from their mistakes. Instead of an *L* for Loser on the forehead, he carries an *H* for Honor around his neck. Some of the people I most admire and honor in my life are the ones who are willing to admit when they have failed. I also seem to lose some respect for leaders who hide, excuse, or minimize their deficiencies or mistakes. Do you want to become a person of honor? Admit, understand, learn, and move on!

This might come as a surprise to you, but Thomas Edison wasn't always considered a genius. In fact, he had reason to play the victim card. His teacher informed the family that Edison was "addled" and unable to learn. Fortunately, his mother, a former teacher, from then on taught him at home. Isn't it interesting how failure can motivate some people to achieve greatness, while in others it's an excuse for mediocrity? The decision is up to you. Remember, just because you failed, that doesn't make you a failure.

Opportunity 2—Failure connects you to people

Then the LORD God said, "It is not good for the man to be alone. I will make a helper who is just right for him."
—*Genesis 2:18*

We were made for relationships. Every time we fail, it's an opportunity to connect with the person God has designated to help you work through it. God operates through others to bring counsel, support, and help in difficult times. In order to recognize who God is sending your way in the midst of your failure, note the following three principles.

1. Open your eyes. Psalm 146:8 says, "The LORD opens the eyes of the blind. The LORD lifts up those who are weighed down. The LORD loves the godly."

Failure means that a door has closed. When that happens, the temptation is to stare at the closed door and refuse to look at other options. That might be your struggle right now. You might be stuck in the question of "Why?" Why, God? Why me? Why now? Why this? While self-analyzing is good, it must come to an end after a while, and different options must be considered. Instead of spending weeks or months staring at the closed door, wishing it could open again, look around and see whom God is sending your way to help you make the transition to a new reality. You have heard it said, "God never closes a door without opening a window." That's true. The fun part is that He will send you someone who can point you in that direction.

When I was in college and single, I was attending a church service where my father was preaching. In mid-sermon, he suddenly stopped. My father proceeded to ask a girl seated in the first row if she had a boyfriend. She said No. He then pointed to me and said that I didn't have a girlfriend and that maybe we should talk. (Embarrassing doesn't even begin to describe it!)

After the service, I went to apologize to the young woman and found myself drawn to this unsuspecting church-dating-game victim. We started going out, and I thought I had found my future wife. Things went well for a while but did not end up well. She broke up with me. As I returned for the next school year, brokenhearted and feeling like a failure, I wondered why God had allowed me to go through that experience. My answer came in the form of a beautiful brunette named Kathy, whom I met during the first week of classes. She became my best friend and for the last twenty years has been my wife. It's the best thing that ever happened to me, bar none. I'm glad I stopped gazing at the closed door and started looking at the open window, with the help and support of Kathy.

You might be going through a similar situation right now in your career, ministry, finances, relationships, or personal projects. I suggest you open your eyes and look out of the window. It's nice outside.

2. Share your failures. Another way of dealing with your failures is sharing them with others. You can do that with three types of people.

Mentors. These are wise people whom you can *listen* to. They have probably gone through experiences similar to yours and can point out some specific ways you can deal with your present uncomfortable situation. Good mentors are hard to find, and they are not the same as opinion givers. There are millions of those. Look for effective mentors. They usually reserve their advice for people who are really concerned about listening and developing an action plan and not just griping about how unfair life is. The operative word here is *listening*. If you do this, you will always find great teachers. Proverbs 12:26 says, "The godly give good advice to their friends; the wicked lead them astray."

Friends. These are caring people you can lean on. They might not have all the answers, but just the fact that you know that they are there for you makes a huge difference. Their purpose is like a steam valve, a point of release for frustration or pain because of the situation. A great friend will tell you the truth but knows *when* to tell you. They are not "yes men," but at the same time, they seldom use the phrase, "I told you so." Proverbs 17:17 tells us, "A friend is always loyal, and a brother is born to help in time of need."

Students. These are the less-experienced people who

can learn from you. Every experience you have had is a lesson that can be shared to encourage, inspire, or warn others. Remember, your responsibility is to share, but you should stay away from trying to use what happened to you to control others. In the desire to help others not make the same mistakes, we can sometimes come across as controlling or overbearing, especially when dealing with people we love, such as our children. God loves us, warns us, and shares with us His guiding principles, but He gives us free will. Extend the same courtesy to others. "I will search for faithful people to be my companions" (Psalm 101:6).

Opportunity 3—Failure helps you understand and claim God's promises

Think about this. Promises exist because failure exists. A promise is God's response to human problems. If there weren't any needs, there wouldn't be a reason for a promise. Let me give you some examples.

Character	Failure	Promise	Result
Hannah	Unable to have children	**1 Samuel 1:17:** " 'In that case,' Eli said, 'go in peace! May the God of Israel grant the request you have asked of him.' "	A child was born soon after.

People of Israel	Slaves in Egypt	**Exodus 3:9, 10:** " 'Look! The cry of the people of Israel has reached me, and I have seen how harshly the Egyptians abuse them. Now go, for I am sending you to Pharaoh. You must lead my people Israel out of Egypt.' "	The people were liberated from slavery.
The human race	Sin entered	**Isaiah 9:6, 7:** "A child is born to us, a son is given to us. The government will rest on his shoulders. And he will be called: Wonderful Counselor, Mighty God, Everlasting Father, Prince of Peace."	Jesus was born and humanity rescued from sin.

These examples are three among many in the Bible. A careful analysis of Scripture shows this pattern again and again:

- Problem—a difficulty presents itself, bringing a problem.
- Promise—a specific promise is claimed in faith through prayer.
- Provision—one leaves it up to God to bring provision in His time.

Why are God's promises so important? Here are three biblical principles concerning the importance of promises:

1. You have to know the purpose of God's promises. Some believe that the purpose of God's promises is only to make you happy. The promises of God are not necessarily designed to take away problems, but to help you deal effectively with them. The promises don't always make storms disappear, but they can always help you travel in turbulent waters. They don't always guarantee to take away evil, but they show that good will triumph. God wants to go further than just making you happy—He wants to save your soul.

2. You have to know that the timing makes a difference. My job is to know and claim His promises. His job is to listen and act, in His time, according to His plan. Some people want to use the Bible as a magic wand, or they think God is a celestial waiter who is just waiting for their orders, so that He can supply their wants. Abraham had to wait twenty-five years for the son who was promised. Israel had to wait four hundred years for freedom. Humanity had to wait four thousand years for the Savior to be born. All were promises of God. All came through. All required patience.

3. You have to know the promise before you can claim it. Because there is a promise in the Bible for each of my specific needs, it would behoove me to try and find out what those promises are, don't you think? We can't claim a promise we don't even know exists. I respectfully suggest that for a moment you stop listening to what other people are saying about your situation and search the Word of God to see what His thoughts are about what you are going through.

Blas Rubio was one of my most memorable church members. He was past sixty years old when I met him. He had been a Christian for only eight years. The life he led before being baptized had been a hard one because he was an alcoholic. His hardcore drinking had taken its toll. By the time we first met, he was going to dialysis three times a week and waiting for a suitable match for a kidney transplant. He was waiting and praying, claiming God's promises for healing.

More than sixty dialysis patients had started the journey with him. A few years later, only five remained. It was encouraging to see Blas's positive attitude, strong faith, and fearless determination as he prayed for a kidney transplant. He took every opportunity to ask for that special prayer request. There were countless anointing ceremonies, prayer-meeting requests, and altar-call responses. One time another member said to him, "Brother Blas, I don't know why you keep praying for the same thing. Maybe this is the cross God has given you to bear." Blas paid no attention and kept praying.

One afternoon at 4:00 P.M., I received a call from the hospital. A highway accident had left a man dead, and he was an organ donor. Would Blas be able to come in?

By midnight, Blas had a new kidney. By 9:00 A.M., he was going to the bathroom on his own. Ten years have passed since the transplant. Blas is enjoying his health and gives thanks every day to a God who keeps His promises.

King David knew the same God—One who is faithful to His promises. He not only knew them in his mind, but he had experienced them in his own life. He knew that Bible promises are God's response to human problems. That's why David could say with all assurance, "Your promises have been thoroughly tested; that is why I love them so much" (Psalm 119:140).

Part three
How?

---

*Understanding the Importance of How We React in the
Recovery From Failure*

Reactions to failure

On my daughter's fifth birthday, she received the usual gifts—some clothes, dolls, a teacup set, a last-minute "dollar store" gift from the guy who completely forgot about the party. You know, the usual. Except for one gift. A well-intentioned but completely misguided party guest brought her a fish tank with three fish. Now I love dogs, dislike cats, and don't care much for fish. If you're a parent, you can identify with me. When your very young children get a pet, you're usually the one who ends up taking care of it.

Not wanting to be rude by giving the fish back or cruel by flushing them down the toilet, I swallowed hard, put on a fake smile, and put the fish tank in my bedroom. By the end of the week, two of the fish were dead. But honestly, I didn't kill them.

The one remaining fish taught us many lessons. The filter broke, and the fish tank became green with algae, but the fish kept swimming. The light bulb went out, and we fed it on an inconsistent basis, but the fish kept swimming. One day I came home and found a white liquid in the fish tank. After I asked around, my two-year-old son informed me that the fish was hungry so he had given it some of his milk. He also threw in some coins so it could buy some more supplies. But the fish kept swimming.

That little fish won our hearts. So we decided to give it a better home. We cleaned out the fish tank, replaced the light bulb, unclogged the filter, removed the coins, and replaced the water, being careful to pretreat the water before placing the fish in it. A half hour after we put it back in the tank, the fish was dead.

Why did the fish die? Maybe it was old, maybe it had a heart attack, or maybe it had gotten so used to the muck and the mire that it didn't know how to react to its new environment.

A big part in the process of transforming your failures into victories is the way you react to them. Your reactions to failure reveal your character and reflect the true condition of your spiritual life. In this section, we will analyze three reactions to failure.

Reaction 1—Quit

> *If your boss is angry at you, don't quit!*
> *A quiet spirit can overcome even great mistakes.*
> —*Ecclesiastes 10:4*

Usually, the first reaction to failure is to quit. A while back, I was watching a report on CNN about an African-American pastor in New Jersey who works with inner-city children. His goal is to encourage and provide opportunities for higher education to as many young people in his community as possible. Although his desire is a praiseworthy one, sometimes his results frustrate him. Reporter Soledad O'Brien asked him a very insightful question.

"How often do you think about quitting?"

He answered in two words: "Every day." He said he felt like quitting at least once daily, but he would wake up the next morning and remember his purpose, and he would decide to give it his best shot all over again. The frustration and pain of failure can do that to you.

Failure causes pain, and since most of us don't like pain, an easy solution is to get away as fast as possible from the person or situation that is causing that pain. It may seem easier, but is it the right approach?

- It's easier to quit on a bad marriage than to work through the issues.
- It's easier to quit a job with a difficult boss than to have an uncomfortable but necessary conversation.
- It's easier to stop attending a church where you had a bad experience than to resolve the problem.
- It's easier to give up on God when life doesn't turn out as you planned than to wait patiently on the Lord.

I believe this "quit first" attitude is endemic in our society. We watch shows on TV that supposedly resolve major issues in thirty minutes. The new normal is the mistaken perception that you can have all of the pleasure without any of the consequences, all of the good with none of the bad, and all of the success with none of the work. The great football coach Vince Lombardi said that the only place success comes before work is in the dictionary. But no one wants to wait for delayed gratification anymore. It's a "make me happy now, or I walk" type of attitude.

The common response nowadays is that when the going gets rough, the tough get going as far away from the rough as possible!

I want you to consider three areas in which people give up:

1. We give up on God. The reason we give up on God, I believe, stems from an incorrect understanding of His divine purpose for our lives. Some think that God's main objective is to make us happy. When that doesn't happen, they think, *Why bother? I mean, what good is God if He is not being good to me and is allowing hard times to happen?* A biblical principle that helped me deal with the age-old question of why a good God allows pain to exist is this:

> God's main objective on this earth is not to make you happy but to save you.

Let that truth sink in for a moment. If you believe

that's God primary purpose is for you to be happy, then when bad things happen to you, you might question God's plan or, even worse, His existence. On the other hand, if you believe that God's primary desire is to save you, then everything that happens, good or bad, fits into His divine purpose for your life. This creates hope instead of despair and brings meaning instead of apathy. You will always have some questions as to why things happen, but expecting trouble helps you deal with it more effectively. Every time pain shows up in your life, you are confronted with two choices: run to or away from God. Which direction are you running these days?

2. We give up on relationships. Relationships are messy. Relationships have their great days, but they also have their rainy, depressing, run-of-the-mill days as well. We have to manage egos, deal with childlike attitudes, have difficult conversations with sensitive people—and that's just your husband. The truth is that sometimes, you and your kin can't!

A long time ago, I learned a short poem that goes like this:

Living in heaven, with saints we don't know, that
    would be glory.
Living on earth, with saints we know, well, that's
    another story.

Relationships are messy. People don't always come

through or stay faithful or truthful. Life would be awesome if it weren't for the people! But we were created for relationships. The devil is afraid of relationships. Notice that in the Garden of Eden, he didn't show up until there were two people, and he didn't attack both, but only one of them. He knows that "a string of three strands doesn't break very easily." He knows that "one can win one thousand, but two will win ten thousand." The reason the devil fights positive relationships in your life is that he understands the incredible power for good that they have. Who are you connecting with these days?

3. We give up on our dreams. People have dreams, objectives, aspirations, and goals. God made us with a specific purpose. Our job is to discover and develop that purpose. What do you do when confronted by obstacles? How easily do you give up on your God-given dreams? Maybe you have dreamed of starting a business, going back to school, changing careers, going into full-time ministry, looking for a compatible mate, or you've had some other dream. At some point, you encountered resistance. As any bodybuilder can tell you, you need resistance to build muscle. You can't build strong muscles with one-pound weights. Have you given up? I encourage you not to quit now. What dream have you given up on?

Walt was a reporter for a newspaper in Kansas City. One day he was called into the manager's office and was fired. The reason given for his dismissal was "lack of creativity." Walt left to follow his dream. Even though many obstacles presented themselves, he never quit. He later became so wealthy that he purchased the newspaper company that had fired him. (Can you imagine how that encounter must have played out? Can you say, "Awkward"?) Walt Disney is a household name today. The reason? He never quit. Neither should you. Join me in repeating the words that Jesus cried out to His Father in the moment when the pain seemed almost unbearable. These words might do you good on a day like today: "He went on a little farther and bowed with his face to the ground, praying, 'My Father! If it is possible, let this cup of suffering be taken away from me. Yet I want your will to be done, not mine' " (Matthew 26:39).

Reaction 2—Blame

Then Sarai said to Abram, "This is all your fault! I put my
servant into your arms,
but now that she's pregnant she treats me with contempt.
The LORD will
show who's wrong—you or me!"
—Genesis 16:5

This verse always makes me chuckle. Let's take a quick look at the story. Abram was married to Sarai. They had no kids. He was old, and she was sterile. Since there were no blue pills or artificial insemination back then, they were pretty much stuck with their situation. That was until God showed up. He promised them a child, and not only that, but He told the surprised couple that their descendants would be so numerous, they would be like stars in the sky or the sand of the sea.

But between the promise and the provision comes that testing time better known as patience. Twenty-five years' worth of it, in fact. Sarai started getting restless and concluded that God needed some help (always a bad idea).

She told Abram her plan. "Abram, dear, put on your hearing aids and come here. Listen to me for a while. I have a plan. I want you to go and sleep with my servant (a younger, better-looking version of me). You will get her pregnant, and *that* baby will be the promised one."

Abram looked at Sarai and said, "You know, this is something very difficult that you are asking me, but I am willing to do it. Not because I *want* to, but because I love you and you asked me to. I'll go ahead and sacrifice and take one for the team." So he put on some Old Spice, put on his best desert outfit, and nine months later, there was a child. Things didn't turn out as planned, however. They seldom do when we try to help God out. That brings us to our text: "Then Sarai said to Abram, 'This is all your fault! I put my servant into your arms, but now that she's pregnant she treats me with contempt. The LORD will show who's wrong—you or me!' "

How?

Notice Sarai's attitude. Instead of accepting and owning her mistake, she transfers all the blame to Abram. That same mentality prevails in our culture today. "It's not my fault. It must be someone else's. Poor me, I'm just a victim of circumstances, a wrong-place, wrong-time type of situation." It's much easier to blame others.

- The reason my kids are estranged from me was not the dysfunctional, abusive manner I treated them, but that kids have no respect for authority these days.
- The reason I left the church is that people didn't love me, the pastor didn't feed me, and the rules got to me, not because I had religion and not a real relationship with God.
- The reason I am in bad shape financially is that I don't make enough money, not that I have a compulsion to buy things I don't need, with money I don't have, to impress people I don't even like.

It's easier to blame others for our predicament. That's why people sue McDonald's for making them overweight. To be fair, there are times when other people cause us pain and suffering. An abusive parent, a sketchy business partner, an unfaithful spouse are but a few examples of real pain caused by people other than yourself.

That might well be your case, and we don't want real victims to assume that they are responsible for damage inflicted on them by others. That being said, there are many instances of lives derailed by self-inflicted wounds.

The actions you must take in order to take ownership of your life, including your failures, instead of blaming other people are the following:

Demonstrate true repentance. This has great impact on your relationship with God. A major step in restoring and growing in your relationship with God is recognizing the basic fact that you are not flawless. In the Old Testament, a specific requirement before a relationship with God could be restored was admission of guilt. Leviticus 5:3 says it this way: " 'When you realize what you have done, you must admit your guilt.' "

In any area in life, a great first step to fixing a problem is to admit there is a problem to fix. We have one big problem. That problem is called sin, which means walking away from God. When we repent, we turn around and start walking with Him.

2. Demonstrate maturity. This enhances your character development. A mature person understands that while you may not be able to control what happens to you, you more often than not can control how you react to it. Blame is seldom an appropriate first response to a crisis or a problem. A mature person doesn't concentrate on spending a lot of time trying to find out who caused the problem, but rather taking the necessary steps to correct the problem. Another way of saying it is this:

- People in denial ignore the problem.
- Unhealthy people complicate the problem.
- Childish people blame others for their problem.
- Mature people find a solution to the problem.

3. Demonstrate humility. That improves your relationship with others. It makes you approachable; in other words, it makes you human. We have spoken at length about the importance of admitting our faults, so we won't repeat that here. Suffice to say that when we resist the urge to pass the buck, it strengthens the leadership of our lives and fosters a climate of openness and grace.

A number of Bible characters demonstrated what to do and not to do in the humility department. One was Nehemiah. Even though he was far away from his people and did not himself participate in the people's willful disobedience, he identified with them when he prayed: "Then I said, 'O LORD, God of heaven, the great and awesome God who keeps his covenant of unfailing love with those who love him and obey his commands, listen to my prayer! Look down and see me praying night and day for your people Israel. I confess that we have sinned against you. Yes, even my own family and I have sinned! We have sinned terribly by not obeying the commands, decrees, and regulations that you gave us through your servant Moses' "(Nehemiah 1:5–7).

On the opposite side of the spectrum was Saul. A weak leader, he loved to justify himself, rationalize his actions, and pass blame to others. When confronted by the prophet Samuel after willfully disregarding a divine command, he said (notice the italics), " 'Yes, I have sinned. I have disobeyed your instructions and the LORD's command, *for I was afraid of the people and did what they demanded*' " (1 Samuel 15:24).

In almost two decades of ministry, I've had in front of me literally hundreds of couples for counseling. I don't recall many times when the husband looked at me and said, "You know, pastor, I am the problem here. I am making a mess in our relationship. I need to love more, hurt less, and learn to forgive always. I need to put down the remote and take my wife out on a date. If you want to know who the problem is, you are looking at it. It's me!" Instead, most couples blame their spouse, Hollywood, popular culture, the fact that they were not breastfed as a baby, their parents, their in-laws, Steven Seagal—anything but themselves. The truth is, we can change and control only ourselves, so let's start there. Leave the rest up to God.

Who are you blaming for your life these days? Maybe the person responsible for at least some of the mess you're in is staring back at you from the mirror. As the old, old song your parents used to sing goes:

How?

It's me, it's me, it's me, oh Lord,
standing in the need or prayer.
Not my teacher, not my preacher,
But it's me, oh Lord,
standing in the need of prayer.

Reaction 3—Rebel

*"Rebellion is as sinful as witchcraft, and stubbornness as
bad as worshiping idols."*
—1 Samuel 15:23

The third way some react to failure is to rebel against God. I define *rebellion* as a lifestyle of willful, constant disobedience to biblical principles and values. It's like Reaction 2 on steroids. I explain it this way.

Imagine you are traveling in a caravan of wagons through the African jungle. Life is not perfect, but there is strength in numbers, especially with the man-eating lions that abound in the landscape. When nighttime falls, the leader explains very clearly the dangers of venturing out at night. You hear him but dismiss his warnings. You are tired of him telling you what to do, when to get up, and where to spend the night.

So you wait until everybody is asleep and go out into the night. Oh, the freedom. No one can tell you what to do now! Suddenly, you hear a growl, and two sparkly eyes are staring straight at you. Any other person would run toward camp, but not you—you're smarter than that. You continue your journey into the darkness. You are free, and you will leave all those lemmings behind. You are in charge now. You are the king of the world!

But that feeling is short lived. You end up hitting some rough patches, and after going around in circles for days, you end up back in camp anyway, bloodied, bruised, and battered, missing some vital body parts, like an arm or both middle fingers. Lesson? Follow the leader. Hang with the others. Stay in camp. It's safer there.

Rebellion is sin. I know that *sin* is not a very popular word these days, but it is what it is. It's not a dysfunction, a disorder, or a syndrome. It's sin. And it can mess you up real good.

A sinful lifestyle will produce the following results:

1. Sin seldom affects only the rebellious one. One of the most common excuses and justifications for sin goes something like this: "It's *my* life. *My* body. What *I* do is *my* business. *My* personal choice. *I'm* hurting only *myself.*" What we fail to recognize is that sin is seldom an individual sport. It is more like a bomb than a bullet.

2. Sin will make you do things you never thought you would do. Take infidelity as an example. I don't think anyone gets up one morning and says, "I think I will ruin my life, lose my family, alienate my friends, destroy my reputation, and hurt the people I love the most by being unfaithful today." Yet it happens—thousands of times every day. Sin is the reason a religious leader is caught with pornography on the *church* computer. It is the reason a senator loses his job by sending racy pictures of himself to women all over the country. It's in the drug-addicted prostitute, the financial guru who steals millions in a Ponzi scheme, the alcoholic father who kills his family while driving drunk, the college student who steals and sells the answers to the test questions. Sin wakes up the reckless gene in human beings.

I have had a chance to speak candidly with several married individuals who were unfaithful to their spouses, and every last one had a common theme to their story. They told me, "I never intended this to happen." Yet it does. They never thought they would "end up like this." Yet they do. Sin will degrade your character, delete your ability for discernment, and demolish your moral compass. Sin will take you places you don't want to go. It's not like a bus, where you can ring a bell and get off at the next stop. It's more like a runaway train, and Denzel Washington isn't coming to the rescue.

I can't count the conversations I've had with people who regret giving in to sin the first time, thinking they were in charge, and now are in a place in their life they never thought they would be. Their addiction, affair, and attraction got out of hand quicker than they could spell disaster. The lesson is, if you don't want to get derailed, stay off that train. Jesus puts it this way (kind of drastic, I know, but hear His point): " 'If your hand—even your stronger hand—causes you to sin, cut it off and throw it away. It is better for you to lose one part of your body than for your whole body to be thrown into hell' " (Matthew 5:30).

His point is simple. Do whatever it takes, but stay away from sin. Even self-inflicted pain is preferable to sin-inflicted pain.

3. Sin will make you stay longer than you want to stay. The problem with a sinful lifestyle is not only what it does to you, but the length of time it does it. Talk to anyone with an addiction, and you will hear firsthand the frustration and hopelessness that characterize their lives. The journey into the forbidden might have started innocently enough, but somewhere along the way a line was crossed, a step was taken, or a decision made that proves almost impossible to come back from unscarred. Is it possible to recover? Absolutely. Is it going to be a very difficult and painful process? Probably. That's the bad news. The great news is that if you haven't started down that road, you don't have to. The good news is that even if you are traveling down that path, you can turn around. Listen to the pain in God's voice as He wonders when His children will turn around: "Why do these people stay on their self-destructive path? Why do the people of Jerusalem refuse to turn back? They cling tightly to their lies and will not turn around" (Jeremiah 8:5).

As you have probably noticed by now, I have painted

a very bleak picture of the reality of a rebellious lifestyle. The reason I needed to, is that I would like to spare you the pain and suffering that is sure to be your travel companion as you go down that road.

I speak from experience. At seventeen, I decided that the "church thing" wasn't working for me and I needed some freedom. My choices were the complete antithesis of the lessons my parents had taught me as a child. I won't spend time glorifying that rebellious past, but my choices were not the best, to say the least. I am thankful to my Lord and Savior Jesus Christ for delivering me from that lifestyle, but I still carry some of the scars, both literally and emotionally. I learned the hard way that there is no such thing as consequence-free sin. There is always a price to be paid, and it's usually higher than you ever imagined.

When I was a child, I heard this story in one of my dad's sermons. I have no idea if it happened or not, but it illustrates a great point. One night a man, let's call him Joe, was entering a watering hole to drink his troubles away. As he entered the cantina, another customer inquired concerning his purpose in the establishment. The man said, "I am here to drown all of my sorrows." After a night of drinking, he stumbled by the same customer, who asked for an update.

"Hey, Joe, were you able to drink your troubles away?"

"No," says Joe, "the little rascals learned how to swim."

Sin promises much but delivers nothing.

One frigid, windy autumn afternoon, my beautiful wife and I were traveling by plane from Michigan to Baltimore. The trip had one stop in Cleveland. The first plane was a sixteen-passenger commuter plane that looked flimsy from the get-go. Anyone living close to the Midwest knows that the winds can pick up pretty good at that time of year. The moment we took off, the problems started. The plane shook violently, the ups and downs doing a number on our stomachs. I started confessing my sins, previous, present, and future, because I thought that the end was near. The pilot's door was open, and I saw him take out a manual that I believe said "For emergencies only!" Red lights flashed inside his cabin. (This was before 9/11, and you could actually see who was piloting the plane.) My wife held my hand until my knuckles were as white as my face. This ordeal stopped for a little while once we got above the clouds, but it started again in our descent into Cleveland. Finally, we made it. Scared, upset, uncomfortable, but we made it.

This experience taught me a valuable lesson. When we were in the midst of that situation, thousands of feet in the air, no one rebelled and said, "This is too uncomfortable, I'm leaving!" The reason was that even though it was bad inside, it was worse outside. You are always safer close to God. Stay in the plane. It's safer there. Remember Noah, safe in the ark: "As the waters rose higher and higher above the ground, the boat floated safely on the surface" (Genesis 7:18).

Reaction 4—Grow

I have not yet reached my goal, and I am not perfect. But Christ has taken hold of me. So I keep on running and struggling to take hold of the prize. My friends, I don't feel that I have already arrived. But I forget what is behind, and I struggle for what is ahead. I run toward the goal, so that I can win the prize of being called to heaven. This is the prize that God offers because of what Christ Jesus has done.
—Philippians 3:12–14, CEV

Just because you have failed, doesn't mean you are a failure. Failure can teach you, but it does not have to define you. A phrase that I have heard or seen in people's lives contains the following word: *feel.* For example,

- "I just don't feel like I can win."
- "I just don't feel that I can love again."
- "I don't feel I can overcome that sin."
- "I feel it's impossible."

Feelings are kind of tricky. It's dangerous to live your life based on feelings and not on biblical principles. The following story illustrates my point.

Before I tell you the next story, I want to let you know

that my wife is the most awesome, incredible, absolutely fabulous cook in the world. Or the galaxy and maybe the universe. (You know, she is reading this book too.)

One night, I was coming home late and hungry. Very hungry. Recently married, I was not expecting my wife to be up, but she was. A feeling of happiness began stirring up inside of me. *Maybe she will cook something for me.* I did not have to ask. She volunteered to prepare anything I wanted. I asked for fried plantains, beans, and sour cream. (Don't judge me, I was hungry!) As she cooked, that loving feeling grew to gargantuan proportions. After what seemed to be an eternity, she came out of the kitchen, a celestial vision like no man had ever seen. Angels were singing the "Hallelujah" chorus and her hair moved in the wind (the fan was on) as she made her way toward me. My heart was going to explode from all these feelings of appreciation and love.

She gave me the food. I prayed a short prayer, the one hungry people pray. Then I proceeded to put the first spoonful of beans in my mouth. You see, there are two recipes for preparing beans. One is beans with a little bit of salt. The second, lesser known one is salt with a little bit of beans. Guess which one my celestial vision used that night? If you guessed option number two, you are correct! I love sugar, but I'm not a fan of salt. The beans were so salty that the Dead Sea took a bite and said, "Wow, that's too much."

I learned a couple of lessons about feelings that night.

How?

It was amazing how fast the adoration was replaced by discomfort. All the time it took for the "loving feeling" to disappear was the time it takes a spoonful of beans to travel from the plate to the mouth. Feelings are tricky. If you make decisions based on them, you are treading on dangerous ground. There is, however, a better alternative.

The Bible passage at the beginning of this section is one I treasure. Paul, no stranger to failure himself, gives us the correct formula for reacting to failure: *Move on.* A look at that passage will bring out several powerful lessons:

1. Paul recognizes his imperfections but does not let them define, stop, or hinder his progress.

2. He understands that the best way to recover from a failure is not to continue to dwell indefinitely on it, but to learn from it and move on. It's very dangerous to drive a car looking through the rearview mirror, and the same goes for your life.

3. He firmly believes that his best days are ahead of him. Victory is yet to arrive, and he lives with a goal in mind. If you know why you run, you'll stay in the race after most have stopped running.

What kept Paul running toward his goal? How can you recover, even thrive, after failing? One word: *grace.* But where can we find grace? We do not live in a grace-filled world. The world does not offer cheap grace. It offers gratification by works. Think about it. We cannot find grace in any of these:

- **Sports.** You play well, you get paid. Endorsements, applause, and fans come to the winner. Sports are ruled by works.
- **Work.** You work well, you get the bonus, promotions, accolades, the corner office, and the raise. Work is ruled by works (no pun intended).
- **School.** You put in the work, do well on your tests, you get on the dean's list. Hard workers usually get the scholarships, the *summa cum laude,* and the parchment paper on the wall that says to everyone, "I earned this." School is ruled by works.

Our world is ruled by works. From the supermarket to the information superhighway, the principle is the same. You get what you work for, sometimes less. It's impossible to buy a car by grace, or a house, or a computer. If you want to go to the mall, get a bite to eat, or get a haircut, come prepared to pay for it. Credit cards supposedly have a "grace period," but it comes with strings attached, usually lasting only thirty days.

The question remains: If we all have failed, and grace is the solution for that failure, where can we find grace? Where is the place where people can experience liberating, transforming, life-changing grace? Once again, one word: *church.*

How?

Church is the place for grace. It's the hope of the world. It's the only place where you can see love for the sinner while he or she is overcoming sin. It's the place people can come just as they are and leave better than they were. Church, with all its imperfections, can be the vehicle that God uses to help His children learn about His grace. I would love to take this opportunity to invite you to church.

- For some, it's already a regular experience. Keep coming.
- For some, it's been a while. Come back. We missed you.
- For some, it will be the first time. Start coming. Don't be afraid.
- For all, grace is bigger than your greatest failure. Come as you are.

"Each time he said, 'My grace is all you need. My power works best in weakness.' So now I am glad to boast about my weaknesses, so that the power of Christ can work through me" (2 Corinthians 12:9).

Conclusion

I would like to finish the book by sharing with you about David, one of my favorite Bible characters. He fought and defeated a formidable opponent called Goliath. I believe that in this story, we can find powerful principles to deal with the people and situations that attempt to stop God's plan from being accomplished in our lives. Simply said, those people are obstacles between you and your victory. Some of those people are well intentioned but mistaken. Some can be family members. Some are acquaintances who share membership in the same organization but little else.

David had been anointed as the next king but wasn't on the throne yet. The present king, a big guy with a small heart named Saul, was in the midst of a confrontation with the nation's fierce enemy, the Philistines. Most know how the story ends, with a great victory of God's people over a mighty enemy that included the giant named Goliath. Before that victory, however, David had to overcome four obstacles in the form of people, all of whom could have derailed his plans. I suggest to you that if you want to become a prevailing, overcoming, victorious person, you need to be aware of these same types of people.

Some would like to limit you. First Samuel 17:17, 18 says, "Now Jesse said to his son David, 'Take this ephah of roasted grain and these ten loaves of bread for your brothers and hurry to their camp. Take along these ten cheeses to the commander of their unit. See how your brothers are and bring back some assurance from them' " (NIV).

How?

The people of Israel were in need of soldiers, not delivery boys. They were in the midst of a war. Did you notice what the father of David indicated to him? "The only thing you are good for right now is to take supplies and bring back news." Even though David had been anointed king, his father still considered him an errand boy.

Whenever God calls you in order to use you, His vision may be very clear to you, but it may not be as clear to those around you! In fact, the ones closer to you might be the ones hardest to convince that you should be doing something different from what you are doing.

The tragic part in the story of David is that the person who tried to limit him was his own father. A word to parents everywhere: Make sure your children know that you are willing to support them. Help them to dream; teach them to stretch themselves. Remember, where one parent saw an errand boy, God saw a king.

It's a good thing David had the sense to "disobey" his dad. The Bible tells us that he went to the front lines and, instead of limiting himself to making deliveries, he got close to the action. He spoke to people, and he observed and analyzed the situation. Then he acted.

Some would like to give you advice (which they are usually not following themselves).

First Samuel 17:20–24 says:

So David left the sheep with another shepherd

and set out early the next morning with the gifts, as Jesse had directed him. He arrived at the camp just as the Israelite army was leaving for the battlefield with shouts and battle cries. Soon the Israelite and Philistine forces stood facing each other, army against army. David left his things with the keeper of supplies and hurried out to the ranks to greet his brothers. As he was talking with them, Goliath, the Philistine champion from Gath, came out from the Philistine ranks. Then David heard him shout his usual taunt to the army of Israel. As soon as the Israelite army saw him, they began to run away in fright.

Did you notice what the people of Israel did every day? The text says they shouted "battle cries." Can you imagine that scene? They would get up in the morning, adjust their helmets, put on their boots, sharpen their swords, strap on their chest protectors, and line up for battle. Probably a leader with a powerful voice would come, and the shouting would start.

"Who will win the battle?"

"We will!"

"Who fights for Jehovah?"

"We do!"

"Who shall plunder the enemy?"

"We shall!"

The only problem was that everybody was shouting,

but no one was fighting. When Goliath came out, their words became as empty as your wallet on the Thursday before payday.

You will find some people like that in your life. They have an opinion about everything, and apart from talking, have done very little else as far as implementation goes. God values our words only when they are accompanied with actions. It is easier to speak about the problems than it is to do something about them.

As I have mentioned before, I love sports. I love to play them, watch them, and coach them. Once in a while, I get together with some friends to watch a football game of the best team in the universe, the Dallas Cowboys. One of the memorable scenarios that will happen in every game is when one of my friends, usually the somewhat uncoordinated, slightly overweight one who was cut from the third-grade flag-football team while in the eighth grade, gets up and screams at the quarterback/coach/defense to do something. He is very confused and/or angry about why the quarterback did not throw to the open receiver or the defensive back failed to make a tackle. I wonder how long my friend would last in the NFL. Probably not long at all. It is one thing to sit comfortably in the lounge chair and pontificate about what players should be doing. It is an entirely different thing to make an accurate pass to the right receiver forty yards downfield with a three-hundred-fifty-pound beast gunning for your head.

A great quote worth remembering:

It is not the critic who counts: not the man who points out how the strong man stumbles or where the doer of deeds could have done better. The credit belongs to the man who is actually in the arena, whose face is marred by dust and sweat and blood, who strives valiantly, who errs and comes up short again and again, because there is no effort without error or shortcoming, but who knows the great enthusiasms, the great devotions, who spends himself for a worthy cause; who, at the best, knows, in the end, the triumph of high achievement, and who, at the worst, if he fails, at least he fails while daring greatly, so that his place shall never be with those cold and timid souls who knew neither victory nor defeat (Theodore Roosevelt).

Some will judge your motives. First Samuel 17:28–30 says, "When Eliab, David's oldest brother, heard him speaking with the men, he burned with anger at him and asked, 'Why have you come down here? And with whom did you leave those few sheep in the wilderness? I know how conceited you are and how wicked your heart is; you came down only to watch the battle.' 'Now what have I done?' said David. 'Can't I even speak?' He then turned away to someone else and brought up the same matter, and the men answered him as before" (NIV).

If it wasn't one family member, it was another. It makes you wonder about David's family. All David wants is to get some information about what is going on, and he can't catch a break. His oldest brother, the same one who was passed over when Samuel went to their house to pick a king, is still angry at him and starts making a scene. What does Eliab really know about David's intentions? How can he know his thoughts? How can anyone know what is in the heart of another person? It's impossible.

Yet we do it all the time. We label people. We assign categories based on race, money, education, family of origin, or church. It is far easier to box people in, to make them fit in these tight little categories, than to get to know them. That way, you don't even have to try to relate to them, because you already know what they are all about.

Eliab belongs to the type of people I like to call "drainers." Some people are natural encouragers, and when you are done talking with them, they leave you feeling better about yourself—uplifted, ready to take on the world. Others, however, have the gift of draining every last ounce of happiness out of your life. Such was Eliab. He could not leave well enough alone. He had to make a comment. He had to make a scene. He had to make sure everyone, including David, knew that David was a nobody, just a shepherd. At a time when soldiers were needed, and rather than affirming the future king, Eliab was judging David's heart. Small-minded people see others as a threat, not as a help.

I love David's response to Eliab. First he asked, "What have I done now?" which shows you that they have had this type of encounter before. Then he did what most of us should have done to that family member or friend who constantly tries to put us down. The Bible says that David "turned away to someone else." People like Eliab you just can't please, no matter how hard you try. Walk away.

Some will try to demand you do it their way. First Samuel 17:38 says, "Then Saul dressed David in his own tunic. He put a coat of armor on him and a bronze helmet on his head. David fastened on his sword over the tunic and tried walking around, because he was not used to them. 'I cannot go in these,' he said to Saul, 'because I am not used to them.' So he took them off" (NIV).

Saul was well intentioned. He was comfortable in a soldier's armor, and he assumed David would be too. But he was wrong. David and Saul were both warriors, but they were very different. Whereas Saul liked the sword, David felt comfortable with the sling. Instead of a spear, a smooth stone; instead of a helmet, a bag full of rocks. Saul didn't make the mistake of stopping David. He just preferred that David not start until he had tried it Saul's way.

We see this same attitude in people every day. We see

it in families. Husbands try to change their wives, sometimes by force. Wives look at their husbands as their projects. Parents try to live vicariously through their children. We see it in the workplace. The old guard is unable to accept new methods and tries to convince and convert the younger workers to "the right way." We see it in churches. Some people try to impose their personal taste as gospel truth.

Now, I want to make something clear. There are some unchangeable, unbreakable, untouchable principles in God's Word that can't be modified according to the year you are living in or the mood of the populace. Those are fewer in number. There are also some things that are just a matter of preference, such as the time to start Sabbath School and whether we should sing two or four stanzas. Do we play the organ or the keyboard? Does the congregation have to kneel for every prayer? What version of the Bible should be used? Those are just some of the millions of details about which good Christians may disagree without being disagreeable.

The problem comes when we try to make people into our image. As an example, I will use styles of preaching. I use some humor in my presentations, because that is who I am. I take my job very seriously, but I have found out by personal experience that humor at the pulpit, when it is done in a tasteful way, breaks down barriers. Invariably, every time I speak, some don't listen to the words but concentrate on criticizing the style. There is nothing wrong with preferring a different style, yet the problem comes when they write notes and have conversations with me (most not very pleasant) about how I should change and be different from the way God has made me. God has confirmed to me that I should not be a generic anyone but be the real me.

To David's credit, he did what many of us probably would not have done, especially at that age. He told the king No. I believe the words he used were "I cannot go." God's hand was in all of this, because David's response did not make the king go crazy (and we know how bipolar Saul could be). My humble suggestion to you is this. Be yourself. Develop your own gifts. Try to be the best you that you can be.

So there you have it. Now you know. Let's go kill some giants.

> David replied to the Philistine, "You come to me with sword, spear, and javelin, but I come to you in the name of the LORD of Heaven's Armies—the God of the armies of Israel, whom you have defied. Today the LORD will conquer you, and I will kill you and cut off your head. And then I will give the dead bodies of your men to the birds and wild animals, and the whole world will know that there is a God in Israel! And everyone assembled here will know that the LORD rescues his people, but not with sword and spear.

How?

This is the LORD's battle, and he will give you to us!" (1 Samuel 17:45–47).

FREE Lessons at www.BibleStudies.com

Call:
1-888-456-7933

Write:
Discover
P.O. Box 53055
Los Angeles, CA 90053

It's easy to learn more about the Bible!